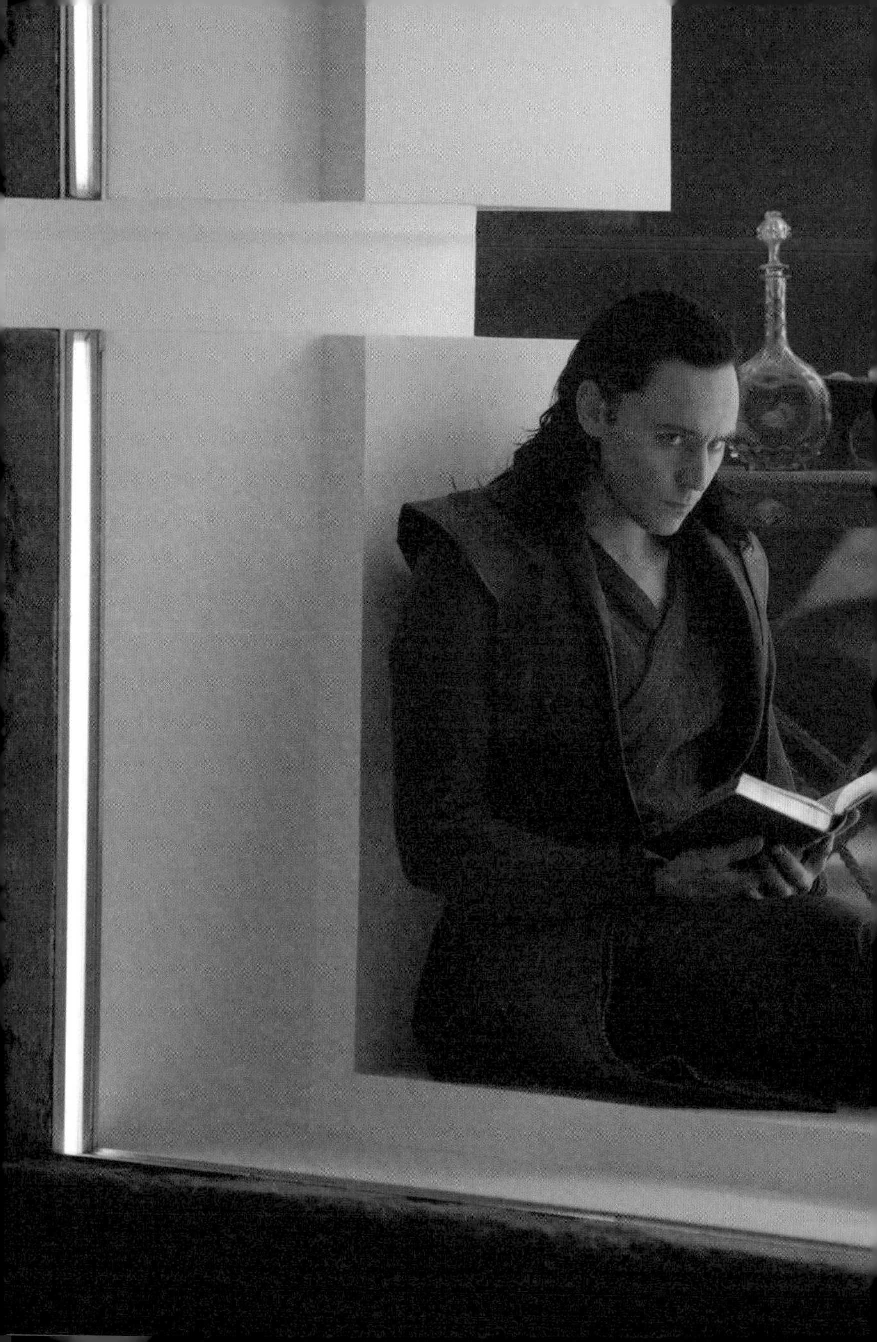

MARVEL STUDIOS

BE MORE LOKI

WRITTEN BY GLENN DAKIN

CONTENTS

MAKING AN IMPACT 4
Be the special one 6
Make a big entrance 8
Talk the talk 10
Confidence conquers all 12
Tell it like it is 14

CLIMBING THE LADDER 16
Stand for something 18
Give clear orders 20
Enjoy the chaos 22
Help others on the way up 24
Know when to move on 26

WORKING WITH OTHERS 28
Praise others 30
Tell people what they want to hear 32
Become a master of sarcasm 34
Use the "helpful" approach 36
Be comfortable with who you are 38

KNOWING YOUR LIMITS 40
Know when to run 42
Face your flaws 44
Know your limitations 46
Know when to complain 48
Don't let others define you 50

REACHING THE TOP 52
Learn to talk tyrant 54
Have all-powerful angst 56
Manage your minions 58
Learn from your past 60
It's your way, or the highway 62

THE SNEAKY PATH TO SUCCESS

You and I wanting a successful career is not that different from Loki wanting to rule Asgard. First you have to make a big impact. Then learn how to work with others—and sneakily rise above them all! Finally, you must somehow end up on top, and enjoy the view from that golden throne. It's easy when you're a god and you can bend the rules of reality a little, but there is also advice here for mere mortals. You too can be an aspiring Asgardian, so why not cross that Bifrost bridge to success?

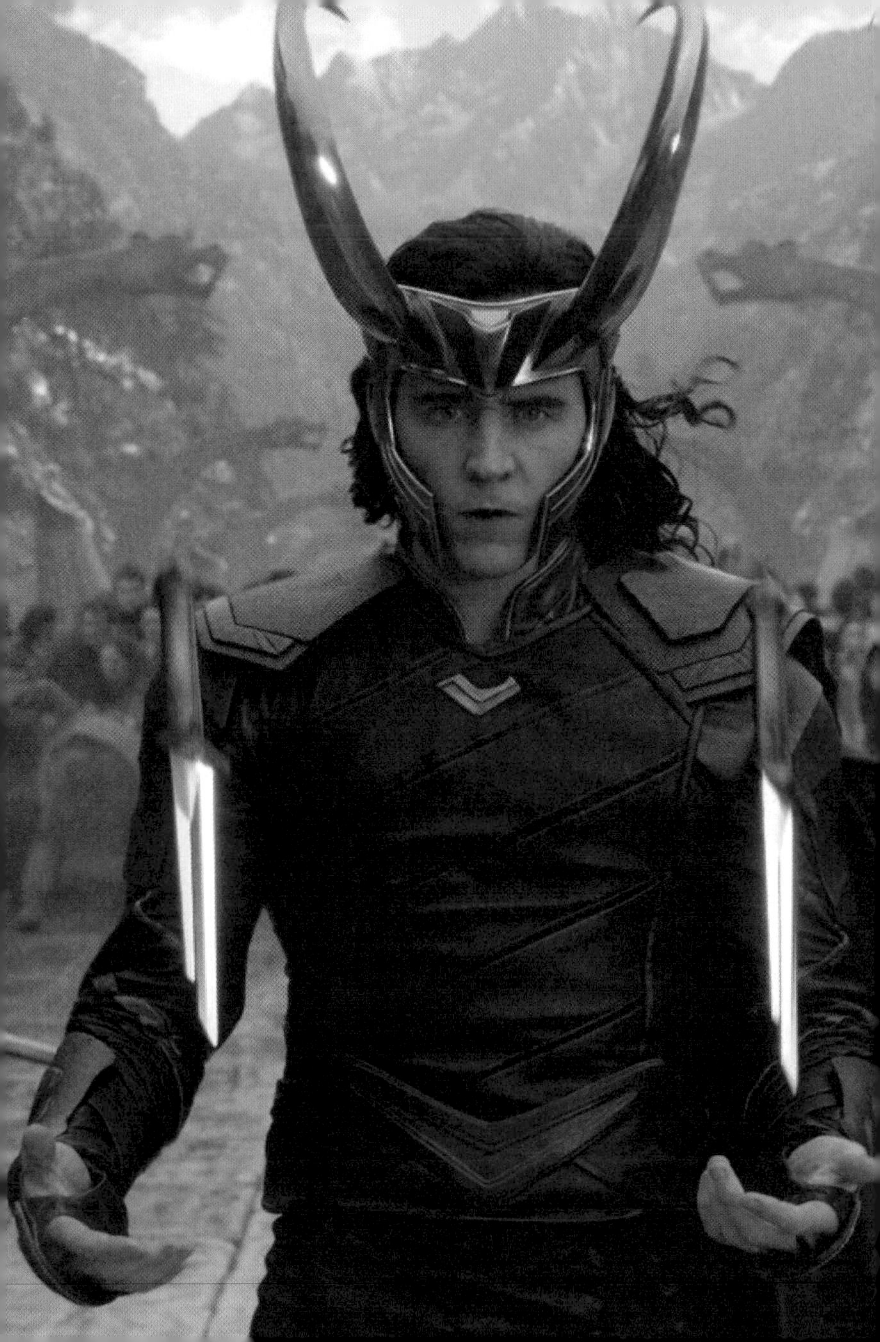

MAKING AN IMPACT

To be successful in this world—or any of the Nine Realms—you need to stand out from the crowd. You can do this with personality and presence, or by wearing a giant pair of horns on your head, as Loki does. Loki knows how to get noticed, and is a natural at standing out (usually because it isn't safe to stand near him). We mortals can learn a lot from the God of Mischief.

"There are no
men like me."
Loki

BE THE SPECIAL ONE

Make it clear that you are one of a kind and you will
seem indispensable. Loki is certainly one of a kind,
as his father was a Frost Giant but he was raised as
an Asgardian prince. When he says there are no men
like him, he is, of course, referring to the fact that he
is a god. But you don't need to have such an amazing
background to stand out, just impress people by
being yourself—we are all unique.

"Your savior is here!"
Loki

MAKE A BIG ENTRANCE

When you enter a room do all heads turn? Learn to make a big entrance and no one will ignore you. Loki does this when he arrives on Asgard to save the locals from the wrath of the Fire Demon, Surtur. It doesn't hurt that he arrives in a great cloud of smoke with an army of Sakaarians behind him. If you can't rustle up such an impressive entourage, you can still make a good start by having something interesting to say.

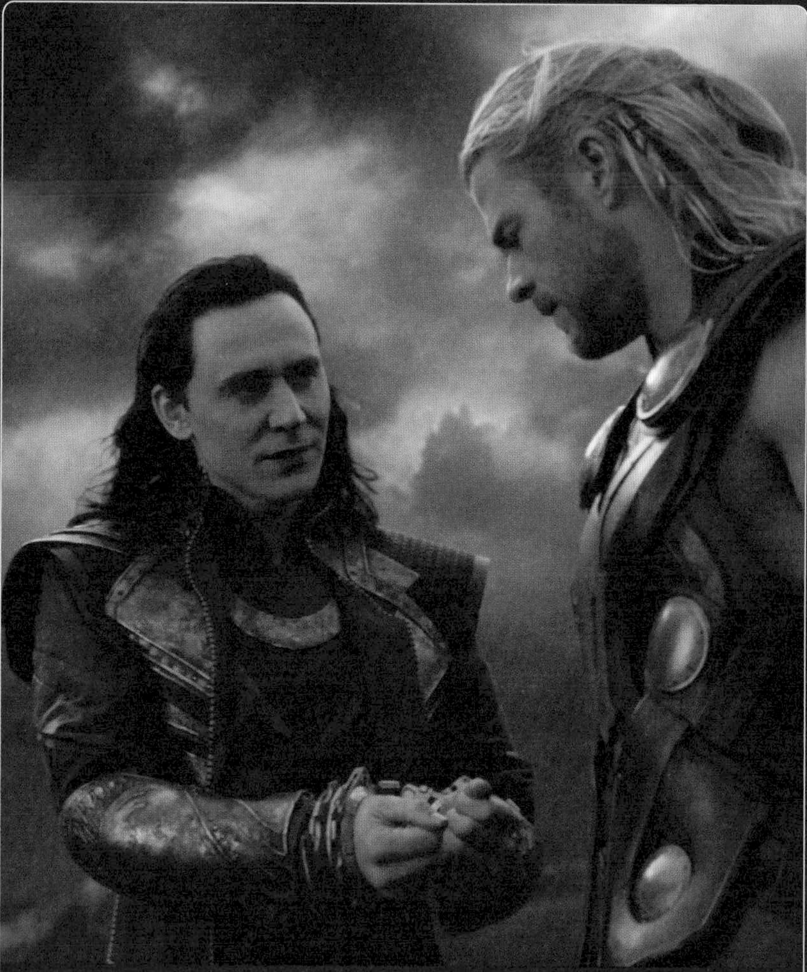

"Trust my rage."
Loki

TALK THE TALK

Making cool and dramatic remarks is vital if you want to impress people. When Thor wants to know if he can trust his brother to battle a common foe, Loki gets past the issue of his personal unreliability by saying "trust my rage." It works. Thor knows that an angry Loki is a vengeful Loki. Keep your big talk short, though. In a crisis, people like to hear snappy one-liners, not your life story.

"Now if you'll excuse me,
I have to destroy Jotunheim."

CONFIDENCE CONQUERS ALL

There is one thing more impressive than doing amazing things. That's doing them with style, acting as if they are nothing. Loki announces he is about to destroy the land of the Frost Giants as if he is about to take the garbage out. Your situation might not be quite as dramatic, but you're much more likely to succeed in your endeavors if you approach them with a whole lot of confidence.

"You will never be a god."
Loki

TELL IT LIKE IT IS

Even for Loki, there are times when only the truth will do. Why? Because the truth hurts, and when faced with someone like Thanos, you need your strongest game. If you have the confidence to tell it like it is, when it really matters, people will look up to you. Some people don't like hearing the truth—in the case of Thanos, he might just destroy you—but it's always the better option in the long run.

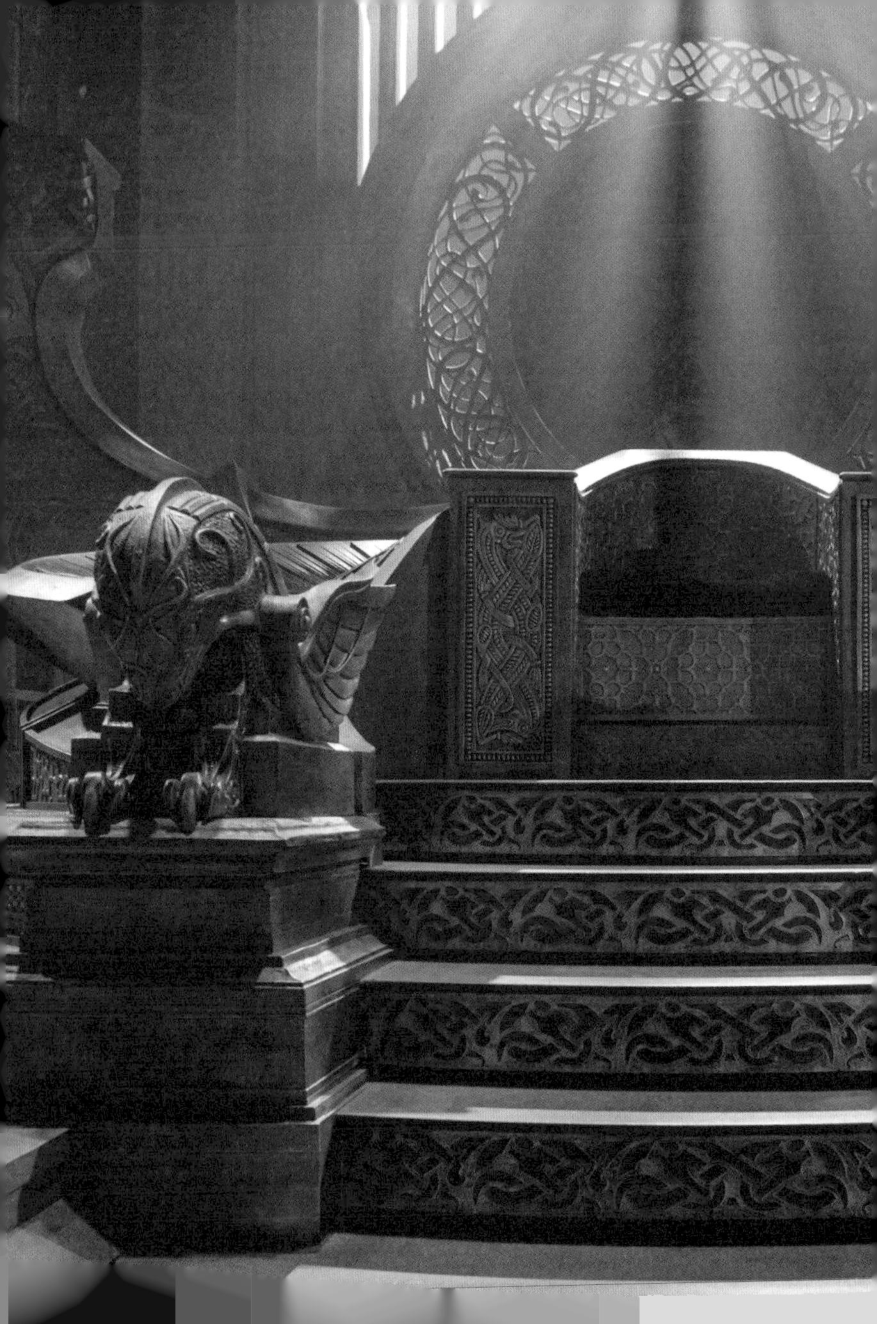

CLIMBING THE LADDER

If you want to rule the world, you need to be smart, tough, and also a God of Mischief. No one ever rose to the top without having a few tricks up their sleeve. You don't need to form an alliance with a horde of aliens, but you may need to do a few deals along the way. It's a long way to the top, but the view of the Nine Realms from there is worth it. And on your journey, a little sneakiness goes a long way...

"I am burdened with glorious purpose."
Loki

STAND FOR SOMETHING

Let's get one thing clear. Rising to the top isn't all
about you. At least that's what you want other people
to think. Loki tells mankind he is ruling them for their
own good. They are better off obeying an all-powerful
god than just vaguely muddling along mortal-style.
In your rise to power you'll need to convince people
you have a higher purpose. It's all about making a better
world... one where you just happen to be in charge.

"Destroy everything!"
Loki

GIVE CLEAR ORDERS

If you want to be more Loki, then you have to get used to telling people what to do. When Loki sends the Destroyer, an enchanted Asgardian automaton, to Earth to punish Thor, he gives it a nice, clear instruction: destroy everything. While it is not very compassionate or kind, it is unambiguous. No one likes a vague order. Learn to say exactly what you mean, and you can get stuff done—perhaps without wrecking half a planet along the way.

"No chaos?
Sounds boring."
Loki

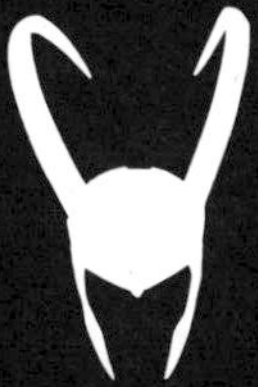

ENJOY THE CHAOS

It's great when a plan comes together, isn't it? But if you stick too rigidly to a plan, then you can be fazed when it goes wrong. If you have a more flexible approach, you can enjoy the mayhem along the way. When Loki is captured by the Time Variance Authority, he discovers that his plans in his original timeline led to his death. So naturally he's in favor of letting chaos take over—it opens up infinite possibilities. Having no plan is sometimes the best plan.

"You might want to take
the stairs to the left…"

HELP OTHERS ON THE WAY UP

You don't have to do this alone. Whatever your goals, there are always people traveling the same way as you. Why should they help you? Maybe because if you are smart you will have helped them first. They say help others on the way up—you might need them on your way down. Loki does not expect to go down, but he will help the Dark Elves invade Asgard if it gives him a chance to betray them later.

"I've never met this man in my life."
Loki

KNOW WHEN TO MOVE ON

Climbing up that ladder isn't easy. It can be sad leaving old allies and friends behind. But if you want to get to the top you have to know when to move on. On the planet Sakaar, ruled by the all-powerful Grandmaster, Loki pretends he has never met Thor before in his life. Well, knowing Thor can have its drawbacks if you're his scheming brother. The pretence enables Loki to stay in the Grandmaster's good books... until it suits him.

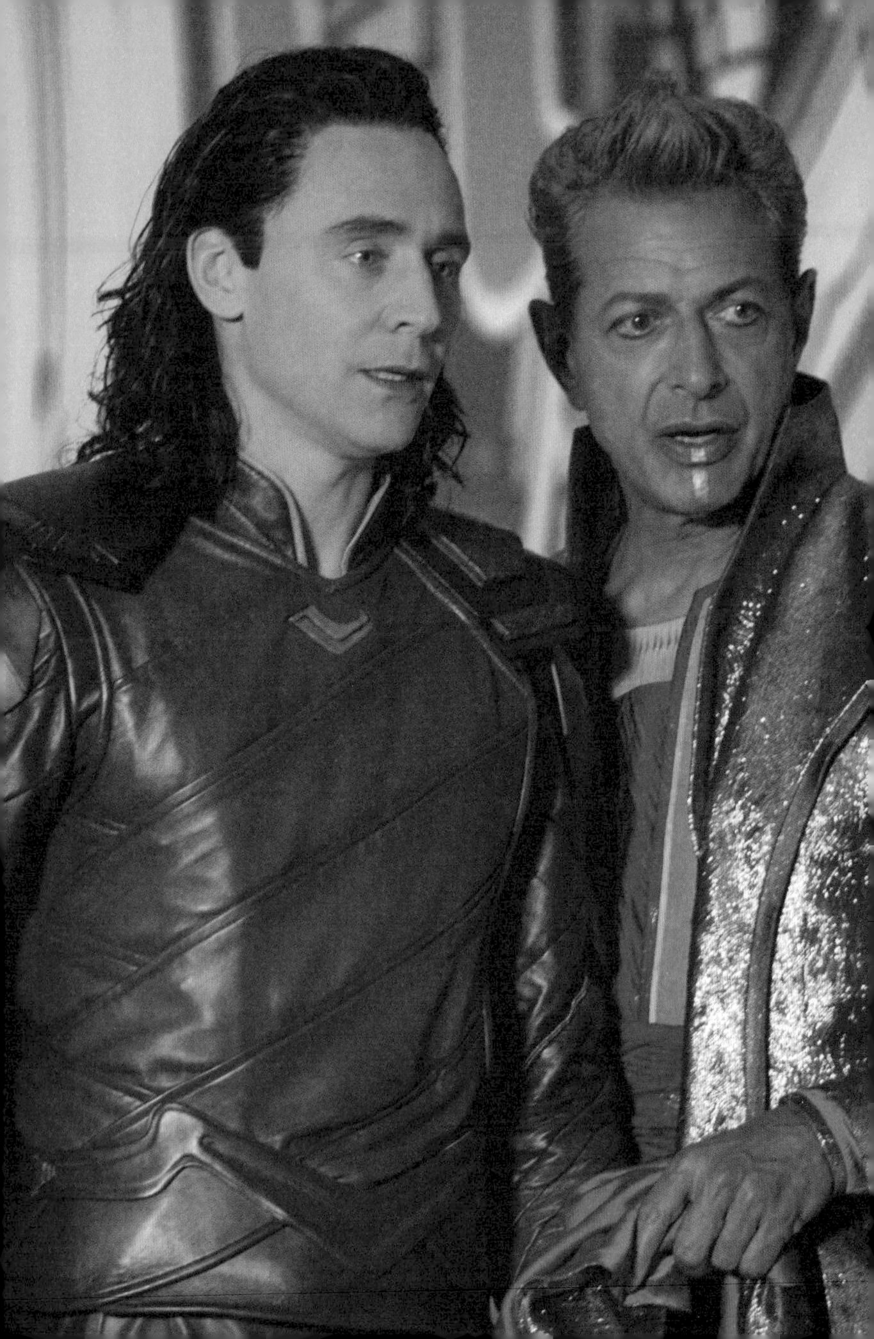

WORKING WITH OTHERS

It is a simple fact in life that you can't do everything on your own. Even gods need a little help from time to time. Thor has the Avengers, and Loki has anyone foolish enough to listen to him... including Thor. If you hone your people skills, you'll be able to convince anyone to help you. Better still, make them think that helping you was their idea in the first place.

"You lied to me
–I'm impressed."
Loki

PRAISE OTHERS

When Loki and Thor escape from an Asgard overrun by Dark Elves, Thor misleads his brother about the escape plan in order to keep the element of surprise. Loki does not mind being lied to. In fact he is delighted to see Thor's sly side, and admits he is impressed. Everyone likes a compliment, so give one out from time to time. Tell someone they are brilliant and they will be inclined to agree with you—and start to respect your opinion about other things too.

"I ask one thing in return. A front seat to watch Earth burn."

TELL PEOPLE WHAT THEY WANT TO HEAR

When working with others, you need cooperation and a good team spirit. This can be achieved by telling people what they want to hear. When deceiving the Dark Elf leader, Malekith, into trusting him, Loki does not offer his services for free. That would be suspicious. He tells Malekith he wants the best seat in the house to see Earth destroyed. That is the kind of bombastic, evil-god talk that vengeful people want to hear. Like Loki, you can benefit from knowing your audience.

"This is a tremendous idea! Let's steal the biggest, most obvious ship and escape in that!"
Loki

BECOME A MASTER OF SARCASM

Telling people they are wrong is not always welcome. Most people don't like their criticism straight—they prefer it blended with kindness or humor. Loki uses sarcasm to get his point across. Telling Thor that his terrible idea is tremendous is a lot more fun, and gets a better reaction. A little bit of humor makes the workplace a happier place—even if your workplace is an other-dimensional battleground.

"Well, you do seem like you're in desperate need of leadership."
Loki

USE THE "HELPFUL" APPROACH

When a ragged army of Sakaarians flees the
tyrannical rule of the Grandmaster, Loki sees
the advantage of having a few helpful stooges
at his disposal. Instead of ordering them around
(they are heavily armed) he takes a sympathetic look
at them and says it is clear they need leadership.
You can take over a situation by making it sound
like an act of charity. And if you aren't Loki,
you might really be able to help, as well.

"Half the fun of being a trickster,
is knowing everyone knows
you're a trickster."
Loki

BE COMFORTABLE WITH WHO YOU ARE

Part of Loki's charm is that he knows he's sneaky, but he's up front about it. Mobius knows he can't trust the God of Mischief... but he can trust Loki to be Loki. He knows where he is with him—which is usually on the cusp of being betrayed. Mobius has to watch Loki closely, but he realizes he can be an asset. Like Loki, be comfortable in your own skin. Then you might get to enjoy some of that God-of-Mischief-style confidence too.

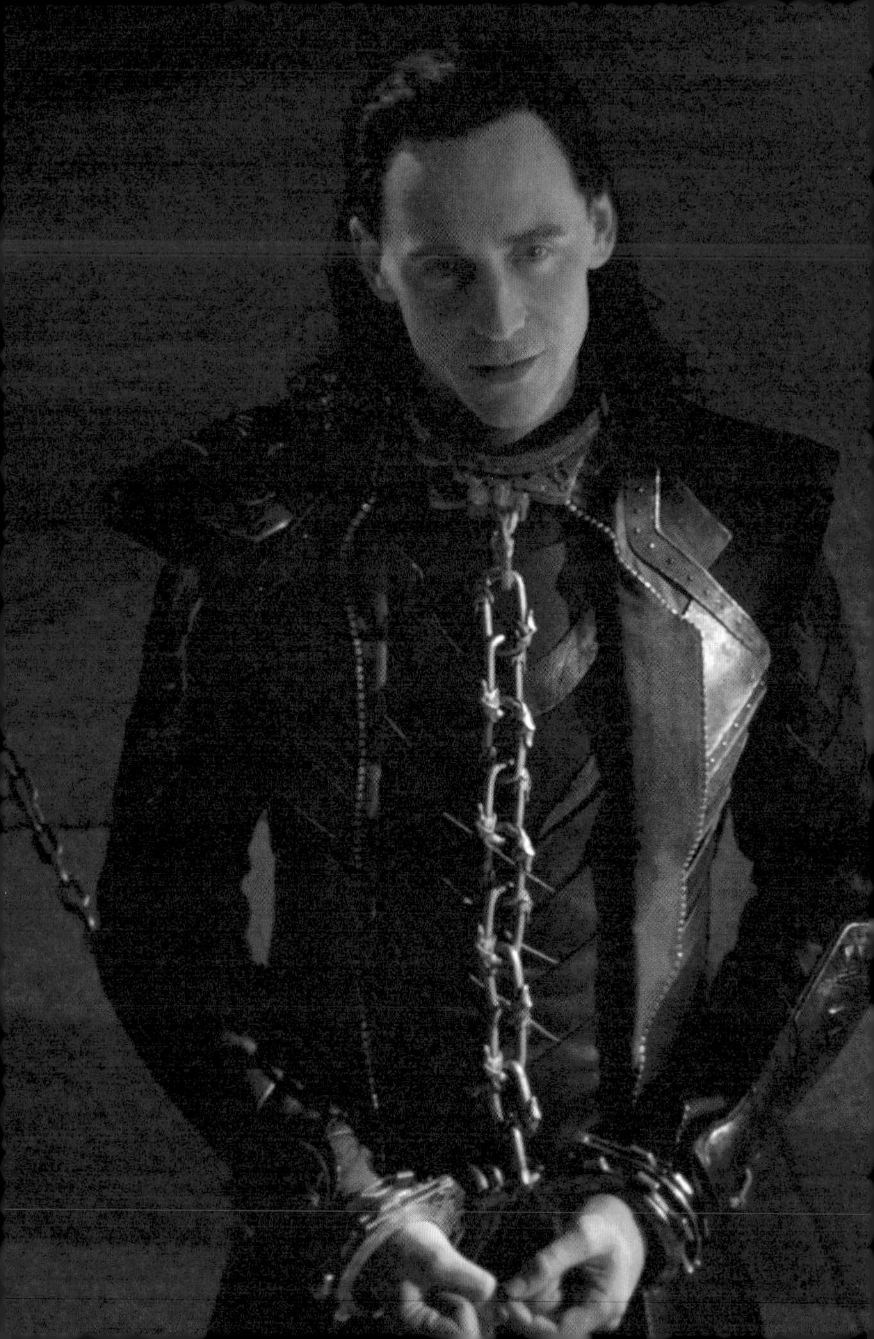

KNOWING
YOUR LIMITS

Even a god knows when it's time to run.
The smart warrior wins some battles and
brings a sick note to others. Only a true
hero, like Thor, will fight when there is
no possibility of coming out unscathed.
Knowing your weaknesses is actually
a strength, as it prevents you from making
mistakes. And knowing the weaknesses of
others will help you negotiate with them.

"I have to get off this planet!"
Loki

KNOW WHEN TO RUN

Have you ever been picked up by the Hulk and
smashed repeatedly into the ground like a rag doll?
No? Well, you're lucky. Loki knows what that feels
like and does not want to experience it again.
As Thor stands his ground against the Hulk in the
Sakaarian arena, Loki makes the sensible choice of
preparing to flee. You might not have the Hulk on your
tail, but some problems need to be escaped so that
you can regroup. Don't be afraid to get out of there.

"You must be truly desperate
to come to me for help."
Loki

FACE YOUR FLAWS

When the Dark Elves attack Asgard, Thor turns to Loki for help. The God of Mischief is astonished. He has many qualities, but let's face it, he is not someone who people turn to in a crisis. But this just might be his time to make a difference. The same goes for you. OK, so you mess up now and then, and you might not always be someone's first choice—but be happy that you *are* a choice. Accept who you are and it will make you stronger.

"I can't see into the future,
I'm not a witch."
Loki

KNOW YOUR LIMITATIONS

Loki has amazing magic powers. He can create illusions, shapeshift, and project energy. He has the strength and durability of a god... but he can get things wrong. He admits to Thor that his plan to remove Odin from power backfired badly when it led to their evil sibling Hela taking over Asgard. He comments that he is not a witch and can't see into the future. Don't let your successes blind you to your own limits. Like Loki, admit you can't do it all.

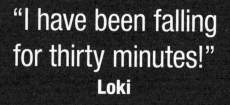

"I have been falling
for thirty minutes!"
Loki

KNOW WHEN TO COMPLAIN

When Loki falls through a portal in the sidewalk created by Doctor Strange, he lands with a nasty thump much later—on the floor of the New York Sanctum. We all like to play tough and put up with life's slings and arrows, but let's face it, there are times when we are entitled to complain! When people push you too far, let them know it. Like Loki, tell them in no uncertain terms what you have had to put up with, and it might not happen again.

"No one bad is ever truly bad. And no one good is ever truly good."

DON'T LET OTHERS DEFINE YOU

Like Loki, you have to accept your limits. But don't let other people tell you what those limits are. Loki is judged by people all the time—usually for the worse. But, like him, you should not let one bad moment or bad decision affect your whole life. We all have the capacity to change. If people write you off, be a shapeshifter and come back in a new way. You will surprise them, and you might just surprise yourself.

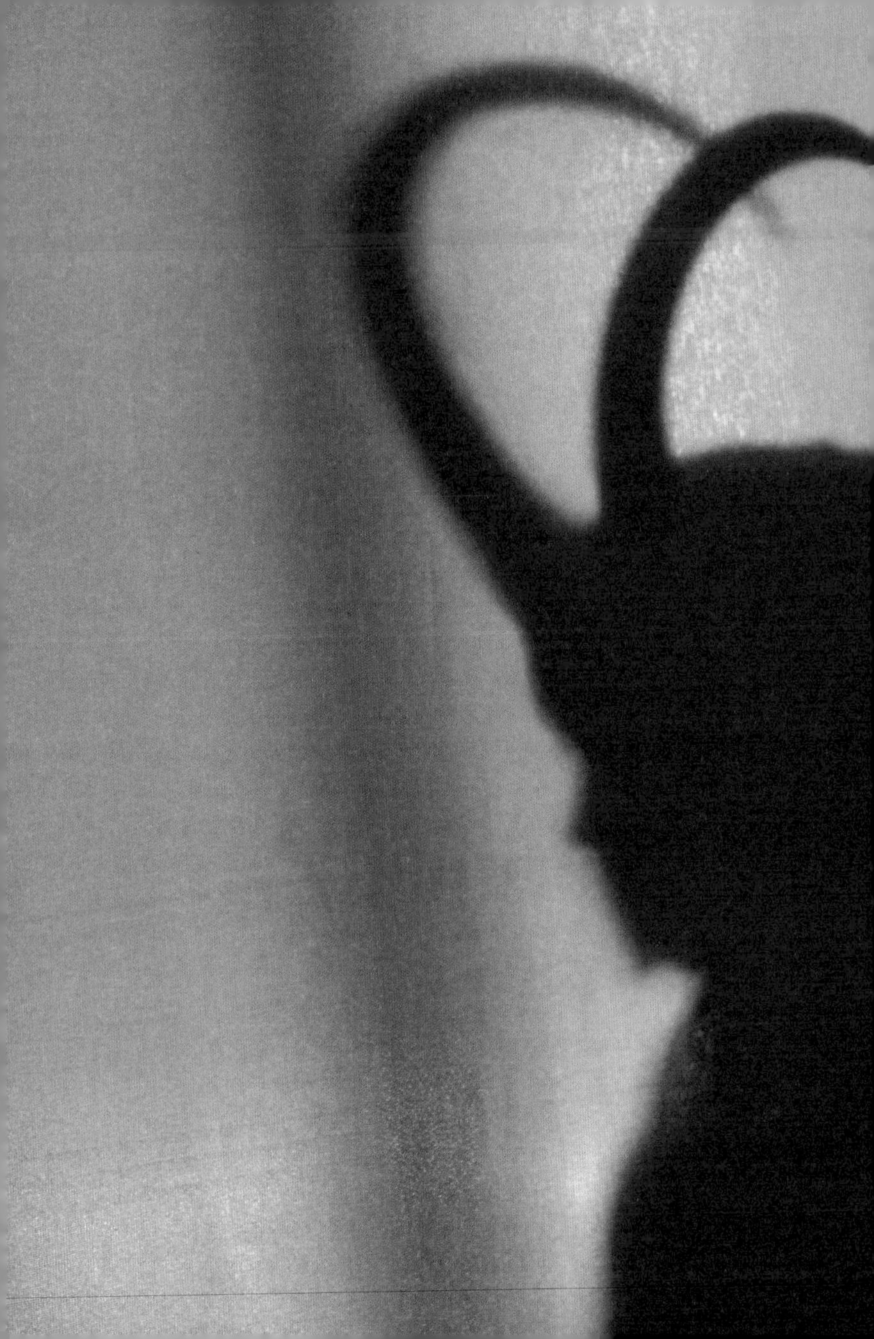

REACHING THE TOP

It's a great feeling when you arrive at the top. But don't imagine it's easy up there. In fact it's just the beginning. Lording it over others takes skill—and yes, sneakiness. The bigger you are, the more people you have to fool into believing you know what you're doing. Ruling Asgard or achieving your goals isn't the end of your journey. It's just the start of a new challenge.

"Kneel before me.
I said KNEEL!"
Loki

LEARN TO TALK TYRANT

It's not enough to just be the boss. You have to sound like one, too. Loki has certain ideas about being in charge, and one of them is that people, especially mortals, should kneel before him. Now he can get away with that—he's a god after all. Here on Midgard, it's better if you just sound assertive and natural in your role. Like Loki, state your ideas with enthusiasm and people will respect your authority.

"The burden of the throne has fallen to me now."

HAVE ALL-POWERFUL ANGST

When you're in charge, don't look like you're enjoying it too much. That will just make everyone else want to be there instead of you. The trick is to give the impression that being the boss is the toughest job in town. Give the occasional sigh, clap your hand to your forehead, and look grim from time to time. No one will want your terrible responsibilities, and you can carry on eating ready-peeled grapes on your comfy throne.

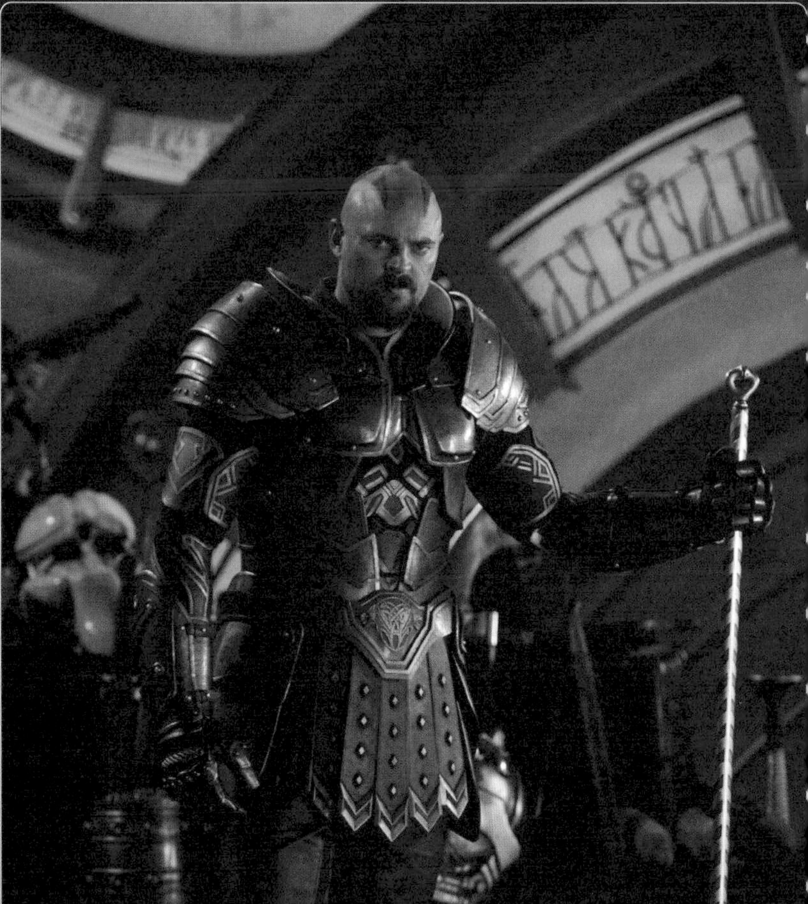

“You had ONE job!”

Loki

MANAGE YOUR MINIONS

When Loki takes over the throne of Asgard, he gets Skurge the Executioner to keep watch at the Bifrost bridge for any return of Thor. When Skurge messes up—well, an angry Thor is pretty hard to stop—Loki is not best pleased. He calls his minion out straight away. This might seem harsh, but being frank about mistakes is better than pretending you don't care, and then holding an eternal grudge.

"I betrayed everyone who ever loved me. My father, my brother, my home. I know what I did, and I know why I did it, and that's not who I am anymore."
Loki

LEARN FROM YOUR PAST

Loki reflects that there is a recurring theme
in his life: that of treachery. He admits he turned
against everyone who cared about him. He didn't
just fall out with his family, on more than one
occasion he actively tried to destroy them. You may
not have such colorful regrets, but god or mortal,
the past can be a painful place. You can either
run from it or learn from it.

> "All of us must stand together,
> for the good of Asgard."
> **Loki**

IT'S YOUR WAY,
OR THE HIGHWAY

So you've reached the top. Well done! This is
your time. But be diplomatic. Don't act like a spoilt
tyrant or Thor will come to topple you. Instead, tell
people that everything you do is for *them*. Every
decision you make is for the good of Asgard.
That way, everyone has to be on your side—for
the good of all! If they disagree, off they go,
over the Bifrost bridge. You are on the throne,
and now... it's your way or the highway.

Penguin
Random
House

Senior Editor David Fentiman
Project Art Editor Stefan Georgiou
Senior Production Editor Jennifer Murray
Senior Production Controller Mary Slater
Managing Editor Sarah Harland
Managing Art Editor Vicky Short
Publishing Director Mark Searle

DK would like to thank: Sarah Beers, Adam Davis, Erika Denton, Sofia Finamore,
Vincent Garcia, Keilah Jordan, Tiffany Mau, Julio Palacol, Ariel Shasteen, and
Jennifer Wojnar at Marvel Studios; Chelsea Alon at Disney Publishing;
and Lauren Nesworthy for proofreading.

AVAILABLE NOW ON VARIOUS FORMATS INCLUDING DIGITAL WHERE APPLICABLE FOR THE
FOLLOWING FILMS AND DISNEY+ ORIGINAL SERIES: Thor, Marvel's The Avengers,
Thor: The Dark World, Thor: Ragnarok, Avengers: Endgame, Loki
© 2021 MARVEL

First American Edition, 2021
Published in the United States by DK Publishing
1450 Broadway, Suite 801, New York, NY 10018

DK, a Division of Penguin Random House LLC
22 23 24 25   10 9 8 7 6 5 4 3 2
002–325110–Nov/2021

© 2021 MARVEL

A catalog record for this book is available
from the Library of Congress.
ISBN 978-0-7440-4453-9

DK books are available at special discounts when
purchased in bulk for sales promotions, premiums,
fund-raising, or educational use. For details,
contact: DK Publishing Special Markets,
1450 Broadway, Suite 801, New York, NY 10018.
SpecialSales@dk.com

Printed and bound in China

For the curious
www.dk.com

MIX
Paper from
responsible sources
FSC™ C018179

This book was made with Forest
Stewardship Council ™ certified
paper—one small step in DK's
commitment to a sustainable
future. For more information go to
www.dk.com/our-green-pledge

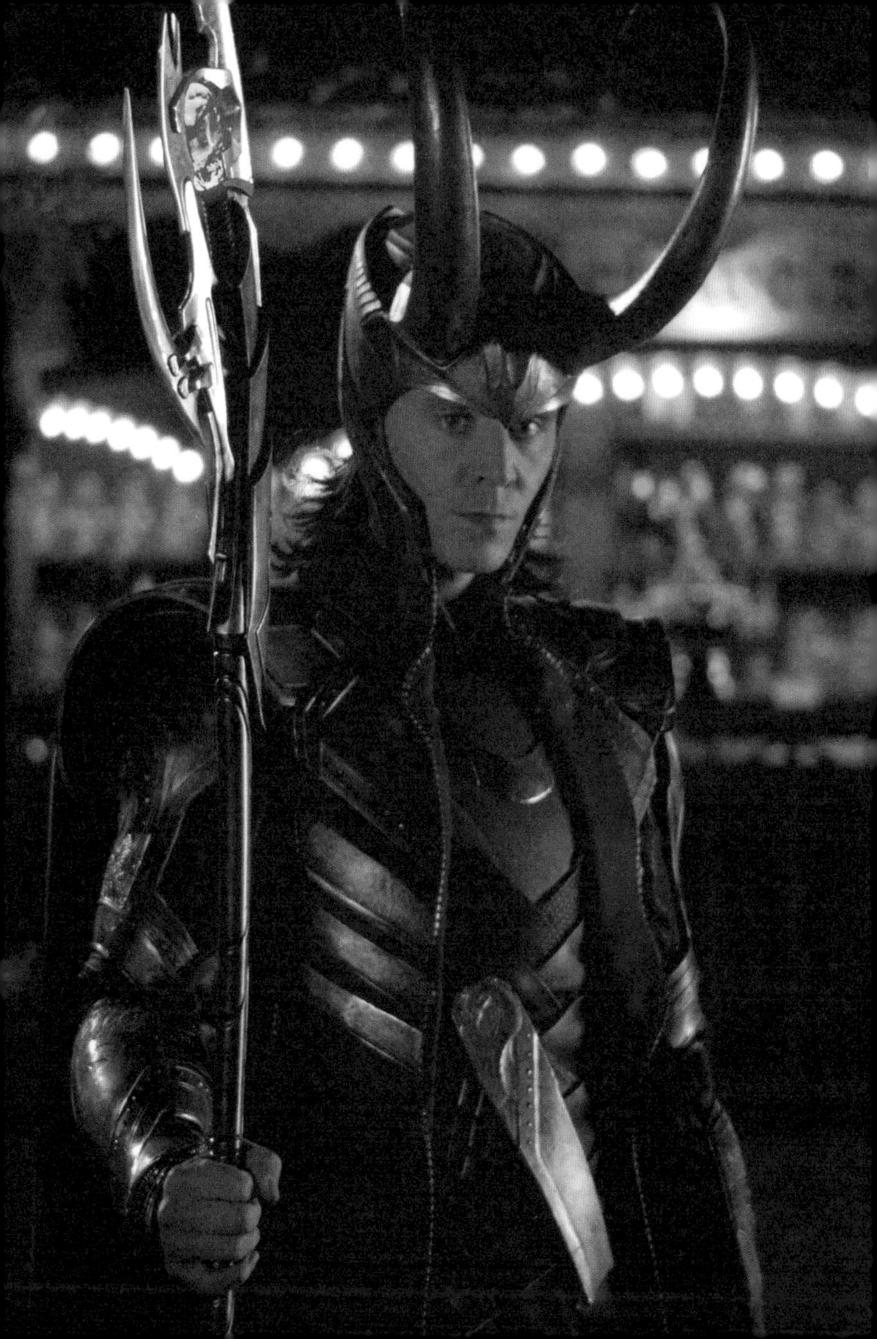

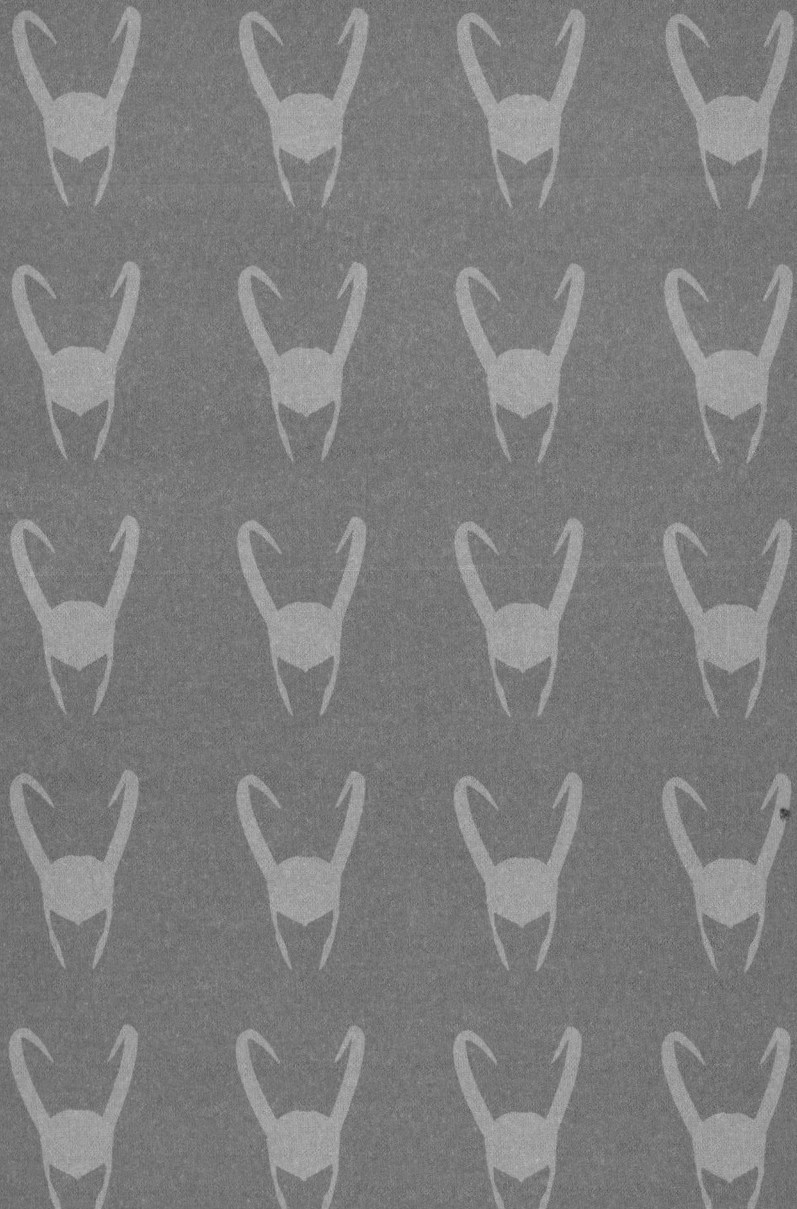